Words From the Heart

Never stop sharing your story!

Ainslee Beaty

BookLeaf Publishing

India | USA | UK

Words From the Heart © 2024 Ainslee Beaty

All rights reserved.

No part of this publication may be reproduced, stored in a retrieval system, or transmitted, in any form or by any means, electronic, mechanical, photocopying, recording or otherwise, without the prior written permission of the presenters.

Ainslee Beaty asserts the moral right to be identified as the author of this work.

Presentation by *BookLeaf Publishing*

Web: www.bookleafpub.com

E-mail: info@bookleafpub.com

ISBN: 9789363311398

First edition 2024

To those who whisper in a world of screaming. You are not alone. You can and will be heard.

Acknowledgements

I would not be where I am today, who I am today, without the people closest to me. My parents, for one. This book would not exist if not for them and they have pushed me to get my work out there. Mom, Dad, thank you, thank you, thank you! As for my brother Graham, he has always been there for when I needed a pick-me up or break. He is the best little brother any big sister could hope for.

There are a million other thank yous I wish I could add, but then I would have to write another book just to accommodate them. My grandparents, for their never ending support (Miss you, Papa), all my wonderful friends who I couldn't manage middle school without, all the incredible teachers in this world like Mrs. Brown and Mrs. Poniatowski, my best friends Av and Quinn for their laughs and love, to my dogs (Now only Henry. Love you forever, Beatrix), and to all the wonderful people that I know and that accept me, no matter how quirky I may be.

Thank you to all the authors whose words gave me wings and helped me soar into my own fantasies. Plus a big thank you to The Write Angle for this amazing opportunity, my endlessly patient editor Priya, and my gifted cover designer Mujtaba. But, also, I thank you, reader. For taking a chance on my book and my words. Thank you for hearing me.

Preface

Words are weird. They flow from pens, yet can get stuck in heads. They can break and build. Hurt and heal. Give voice to silence. But for all the contradictions, one thing is certain. Words are powerful.

Moments

There in a second,
Just as fast... gone.

A quick and happy beat,
Like a catchy song.

A fleeting yet resonating flash,
Like echoing thunder.

An unstoppable instant,
A wave forcing you under.

A simple, sincere word,
Like wind under a wing.

All so fast, all so small,
Yet they.
    Mean.
        Everything.

Heart of Stone (Part 1)

"You have a heart of stone," they say,
Because they can not see my tears,
That trickle down deep inside,
To water my hopes and my fears.

"You have a heart of stone," they say,
Because when I speak, my words recede,
My garden whispers to my mind,
That paper is what I really need.

"You have a heart of stone," they say,
Because I don't feel how I should,
As their words shake my garden's trees,
Cracking stumps and snapping wood.

"You have a heart of stone," they say,
And I wonder if they're right,
If my garden really is just rock,
No blossoms, no growth, no light.

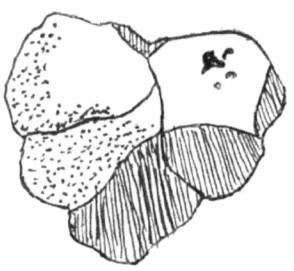

A Bird in Flight

The breeze beneath me,
Wings open wide,
Soaring to the sun,
Cloud and feather side by side.

Could fly forever,
With the wind and the sky,
Forever in this moment,
Just the stars and I.

But then the wind stops,
And my ears start to pop,
The sun and stars call,
As I stutter and fall.

Back down to the Earth,
And the dangers on the ground.
Back down to the Earth,
Where I crash without a sound.

My wings are clipped,
My feathers are plucked,
I'm branded by the Earth,
Yet I am not stuck.

Palindrome

You're at peace.
Calm descends
Everything fits
Just for a moment
You're ready to face anything
Until you're not.
You're timid and scared
Shadows yawn underneath
Like inky tentacles
Your breathing comes fast
You gasp and shake
Worries invade every thought
You're at war.

Where You Belong

So many people,
In this *very* big place,
So many worlds,
Spinning through space.

And so many groups,
People who just click,
Friendships that took time,
And can't help but stick.

But there's always an odd one out,
Always one remaining,
Looking for a place to belong,
Searching, grasping, straining.

Yet that part is not true,
That stanza's a lie,
Everyone can feel that way,
Deep down inside.

So when you feel so alone,
Remember you are unique,
And everyone doesn't have to fit in,
Sometimes you are what you seek.

I'm possible

Impossible:
Very unreasonable,
Not able to be done,
Not real or unfeasible.

Yet this word,
So final and unkind,
Has another form,
One you must look to find...

I'm possible: doable,
There's a chance; it can be done,
Just keep on trying,
If you do that, you have won.

Impossible: unthinkable,
Hopeless; unattainable,
I'm possible: perseverant,
Hopeful; uncontainable.

Funny how close,
These two opposites are,
Like seeing a ball of gas,
And looking at a star.

You're Not Alone

You can be worried and scared,
Called on but not prepared,
Laughed at for what you wear,
But you're not alone.

You can be stuck in your grief,
Losing all your belief,
Start drifting like a leaf,
But you're not alone.

You can be encased in walls,
That never seem to fall,
Making you feel small,
But you're not alone.

You can be trapped in your mind,
Lost and left behind,
Caged and confined,
But you're not alone.

No matter how...
dumb.
unloved.
untethered.
weak.

sad.
ALONE you feel,
Know that other people feel like that too.
And even more people want you to feel...
connected.
cared for.
brave.
smart.
supported.
strong.
and LOVED.
Although healing won't happen overnight,
That doesn't mean it never will.

You are never alone, and never will be.

Why?

So many questions,
Swirling and dancing like snow,
So little answers,
Leaving the future unknown.

Why?
Why is kindness not our focus?
Why?
Why do we feed on anger like locusts?
Why?
Why do we as people fight?
Why?
Why do we have to be right?

So many questions,
Swirling like snow,
So little answers,
But some I know.

I know kindness is important,
Although sometimes unseen,
It does make a difference,
That you can find if you're keen.

I think that anger comes quick,
It's harder to be calm,
Happiness takes grit.

We fight because of something,
That happened in the past,
Now we must move on to peace,
And work to make it last.

But why must we be right?
Because we fear being wrong?
Like if we mess up or fail,
We would not look quite as strong?

It takes courage to fail,
To admit you're not right,
To say you DON'T have the answers,
But you'll shine just as bright.

Lavender

I remember that day,
When the trees whispered our names,
And the sun watched us from up high,
The clouds crawled across the sky,
The sunflowers strained to reach the sun,
The bees murmured buzzing thoughts,
The birds called down from the branches,
The squirrels chased each other up the trees,
The grass danced in the billowing breeze,
The flowers flounced their bright reds and golds,
And the fields of lavender stretched on and on,
Rustling and singing their quiet songs.

When You Look at a Pencil

When you look at a pencil,
Sometimes all you will see,
Is a stick full of rock,
No possibility.

But it's not just wood and stone, It puts your
thoughts in your hand,
Breathing life onto paper,
It can help you take a stand.

From writing thrilling tales,
To making music and art,
Each pencil stroke is pure,
Because it comes from your heart.

Rainbow

You must see all the colors,
To find the rainbow.

Breathe

Invisible walls,
Closing me in,
Leaving no escape,
Trapped.

An inner python,
Encircling my neck,
Cutting off all breath,
Wrapped.

A million eyes,
Staring and judging,
Until I can't take it,
Snapped.

Bubbling and boiling,
I could run to the moon,
Fueled by need,
To get away,
From unscalable walls,
Relentless snakes,
Prying eyes,
No escape,
Stuck.
All of it sticks in my throat,

Like a bursting pipe,
I can't–

Breathe.
A voice reminds me,
Breathe.

Tears

Rivers down my cheek,
Water saying what words can't.

Perseus and Medusa

Grew up in the house of wisdom,
Athena, my teacher,
My mother, my guide,
But now I go alone,
Carrying my desperate pride.

Snakes as hair to tame,
A curse upon my name,
Athena was my everything,
Until she made me nothing,
A lesser being,
A monster.

I must slay the beast,
Woman of snakes and stone,
All because I fought to prove,
That the rich and royal were wrong,
That I was worthy,
That I was something…
And I will.

If it's a monster she wants,
It's a monster she'll get.
The world made me a reject,
So now they shall regret,
Freeze under my gaze,

The legend I will raise,
Take my life and my power…
Until I take it back.

I will take Medusa's head,
Toss it at their gilded feet,
Showing that I'm right,
The world laughed in my face,
But soon I'll be the one laughing.

I could have been more,
Before the world took my heart,
And turned it to stone.

My enemies will cower,
As I show them my power,
Be warned.

My enemies will cower,
As I show them my power,
Be warned.

I'm Perseus,
And I'm the hero.

I'm Medusa,
And I'm the monster.

Sunday Afternoons

Nothing to do,
Nowhere to go,
No rushing, no busy,
Hurrying? No!

Just us and the clouds,
Firepit crackling,
Sweaters and blankets,
Blue jays cackling.

Just us and the music,
Acoustic guitars strumming,
Drums gently booming,
Chris Stapleton humming.

Just us,
Right here,
Right now.

Cicadas

G entle, fluttering wings,
R oaming the trees' canopy,
O h, what a lovely sound,
S ignaling summer,
S leeping for 17 years.

I just wish they would shut up.

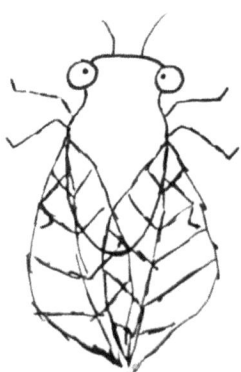

Not Enough Words

Sometimes there are too many words,
An ocean's worth of letters,
And sometimes you start drowning,
Sinking past 'I'm sorries' and 'feel betters'.

Other times words are elusive and lost,
Flapping like birds just out of your grasp,
They get stuck deep in your throat,
Closing it like a coat and a clasp.

Words can be elusive, tricky, or lost,
But they are also beautiful and strong,
They can change a whole nation,
Or just right a simple wrong.

Beatrix

Dogs are perfect.
Especially the…
Cheese puff stealing,
Fire pit loving,
Flower eating,
Queens.

Miss you, Bea.

Junco

The junco is not,
A well-known bird,
Really is 'junco',
Even a word?

It's a small backyard bird,
Gray and white,
Comes out in winter,
After an autumn flight.

It's not the fastest,
It can't fly for that long,
Not the most colorful,
Not the prettiest song.

But the junco keeps flying,
Keeps strutting its colors,
Keeps singing and soaring,
Among all the others.

The other birds may be pretty,
Or fast or loud or strong,
But the junco is unique,
So it sings its OWN song.

Dogs

Sweet little nose,
Preciously perky ears,
Wet, pink tongue,
Licking away my tears.

Swishing, swiping tail,
Perfect baby paws,
Silky, soft fur,
Beautiful just because.

Deep, soulful eyes,
Seeing all of you,
'Man's best friend',
Was never more true.

Boundless, endless love,
No hate, no sad, no stress,
Fearless, flawless friend,
To them, you're never 'less'.

Hear Me

If a star is shining,
But nobody sees,
Does it still shimmer?
Or does it just freeze?

The Storm

Clouds are brewing,
Humid and warm,
Thunder starts pounding,
A vicious storm.

Words fly like lightning,
Unhinged but unbound,
Rain batters and bashes,
I shiver at the sound.

Eventually, it tires,
Packs up and moves on,
Leaving only the wind,
Wailing a sad song.

But better to be sad,
To be drenched by the sky,
Than to be comfy and soft,
Wrapped up in a lie.

Stuck

My throat starts to close,
Trapping my words inside it,
And nothing comes out.

Daydreams

When people get tired,
They drift off to space,
Traveling to new planets,
Or some other place.

Going on adventures,
Exploring new lands,
When you just can't focus,
Your brain gives the command.

All systems check,
Seven, six, five, four…
It's time for take-off,
For the dream to leave the floor.

Although you must focus,
That is crucial and vital,
Find time for a break,
And let your brain dream by the mile.

Palindrome 2

You can do it.
Step after step
Keep climbing, keep going
You're almost there
You try so hard
Can you make it?
Every step hurts
It's all too much
The pain, the sweat, and the tears
You can't do it.

Invisible

Can you see me?
Fading and falling,
Silenced and silent,
Unseen and unheard,
Even if I try,
Sometimes all you see,
Is the wall behind me.

Dear You…

Dear You,

Hi! Hola. مرحبًا. Witam. 你好.
This goes out to you.
Life is hard.
We all know that's true.

You might be young,
You might be old,
You might be poor,
Or rich in gold.

You are still human.
You and everyone around.
So what if you're different?
'Normal' has yet to be found.

You are still treasured,
Even if you can't see it,
You are still loved,
Even if you can't feel it.

The Race

At thirteen, I decide,
To enter a great race,
At the end? A secret prize,
A prize that I would chase.

I speed down the track,
Always looking ahead,
If I stop or if I stumble,
My win's as good as dead.

Trees and buildings blur,
Faster, smarter, stronger,
There will be something better down the line,
If I hang in a little longer.

I leap over hurdles,
I jump and twist and spin,
I don't care about the run,
I just want to win.

I'm given the prize,
They say I did it, that I won,
But then I look around,
And realize what I've done.

I'm alone.
I won the race, but who was I racing?
I sped past everything,
For the fantasy I was chasing.

The prize itself is simple,
A mirror rimmed in gold,
And as I stare at a stranger,
I miss that thirteen-year-old.

Origami

With every new fold,
The paper starts to transform.

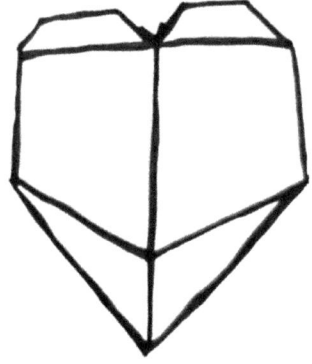

Labyrinth

The labyrinth of middle school,
Constantly changing,
No one's maze is the same,
It's always rearranging.

Take a turn to the right,
And fall into a pit of thorns,
Take a turn to the left,
And meet the Minotaur's horns.

There's no magical rope,
No golden thread,
Find your way out yourself,
But watch where you tread.

Pass lockers and doors,
Dodge the occasional fight,
Through gym and math,
Day after day and night after night.

Suddenly… you're out,
The walls fall away,
Because this adventure is over,
The next starts today.

How To Human

Step One: Breathe.
Humaning can be hard,
Side effects include anxiety,
The inky black feeling,
Rippling through our society.
It can also include:
Rage, sorrow, confusion,
But to successfully human,
Breathing is the solution.

In… out…

Wings of Words

Clouds float past,
Their droplets tickle my face,
Fluff spins around me,
I'm flying towards space.

The ground falls away,
I race higher and higher,
Past planes and jets,
Yet I will not ever tire.

I soar on my wings of words,
Each page sends me up and up,
Ink and paper swirl,
I'm transported to world after world,
Watching lives unfurl,
Seeing love and hate,
Hope and sorrow and wonder,
Galaxies upon galaxies of beauty,
Villains and heroes,
Meteors and nebulas,
Characters and conflict,
Planets and stars,
It's galactically, impossibly, indescribably…
Beautiful.

Teenagers

No longer a child,
But not an adult.
Stranded in the middle,
Of young and old,
Of 'grow up' and 'enjoy your youth',
A swirl of hormones and high school,
That spits us out at the end,
Seven years 'older and wiser',
'All grown up' and 'moving on',
…Well, someday.

For now, I'll just be thirteen,
Still enjoying my youth,
Still growing up,
Still a teenager.
I might be stuck in the middle,
But maybe that's okay.

Hope

Hope is a river,
It is power and strength,
As it rushes,
Seaward.

Fear it you may,
But if you fight the current,
You will never move,
Forward.

To let go, you must trust,
And only then will you see,
People drifting alongside you,
Knowing not where they will end up,
Knowing the pain they have lived, yet,
Knowing they can't go,
Backward.

Hope is a river,
Follow it to tomorrow,
It's the river of life,
So sail on.
And then that hope will carry you:
Onward.

Words From My Heart

When my heart cried,
I ignored it.
When my heart spoke,
I misheard it.
Now though…
When my heart cries,
I tend to it.
When my heart speaks,
I listen.
And I share its words.
Because my heart has a lot to say.
And its words hold power.
So I let my heart speak.
And I listen,
Hoping the world will too.

Heart of Stone (Part 2)

Until I hear a CRACK,
As the rock starts to shatter,
And just like that, I realize,
Their words don't matter.

My garden bursts forth,
Different, weird, and proud,
No stone walls can hold me,
I'll be quiet, I'll be loud
I'll be shy, I'll be brave
I'll be growing into ME.

So bring your words of steel,
Call me "heart of stone",
Test me, and you'll see,
All the seeds I have sown,
All the light I have shone,
And all the ways I have grown.

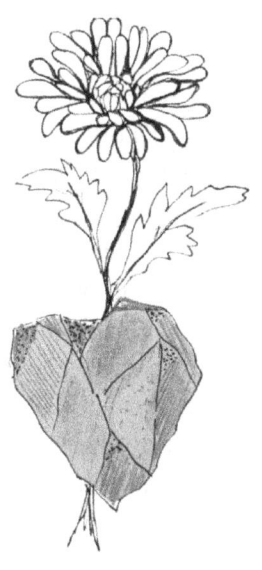

Afterword

This book is a culmination of my poems from the last few years. I started writing poetry back in fifth grade, and during indoor recess I would sit quietly at my desk and just jot down ideas in my notebook. I started to get more into poetry as I entered middle school, using it as an outlet for my feelings. Eventually, I started to share them with my parents. My mom always pushed me to share them with others, but I never knew how or when. That's when I found Bookleaf Publishing at the end of seventh grade and got the idea to write this book that is in your hands. It's taken months to piece together this messy mosaic of love, truth, and hope. I hope that if you love to write like me, you follow that. Or if you have a passion of your own, cultivate it. Let it grow and bloom into something beautiful that makes you happy. But don't keep it in the dark; share your masterpiece with others and let it make them happy too. And that's how we can grow as people.

Printed in the USA
CPSIA information can be obtained
at www.ICGtesting.com
LVHW021437031124
795577LV00021B/161

9 789363 311398